20 words

Benchmark Reading

Starter **1**

Benchmark
EDUCATION
Building Literacy and Language for Life ™

Introduction

Word Chant

This helps learners become familiar with the key words.

Phonics

This helps learners focus on a special sound.

Get Ready

This section introduces the content of the unit with a related picture and a question to stimulate learners' interest.

Key Words

This section introduces the unit's key words.

Sight Words

This section provides words that learners should be familiar with and able to read.

Reading Passage

The reading passage presents various fiction and nonfiction texts with illustrations and pictures.

Focus

This question helps learners know what to focus on while reading.

Check

Learners can quickly check their understanding.

Story Song

Learners can enhance their reading and speaking skills with the story song.

Find & Draw
Learners can find the unit's sight words in the reading passage.

Phonics Chant
Learners can learn the sounds of letters.

Write & Read / Read & Circle
Learners can practice writing or reading the sounds of letters.

Build Language
This section presents the main sentence pattern in the passage with the chant. Learners can also practice the sentence pattern by tracing the sentence.

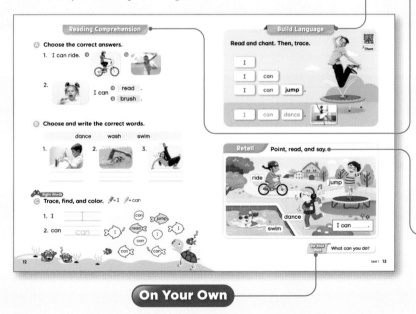

Reading Comprehension
Ⓐ This section provides reading comprehension questions. Learners can check how well they understand the passage by solving questions.

Ⓑ Learners can practice reading and writing the unit's key words.

Ⓒ Learners can practice reading and writing the unit's sight words.

Retell
Learners can retell the passage by pointing at or numbering the pictures.

On Your Own
This section allows learners to think about their own experiences with the unit's topic.

Workbook
The workbook enables learners to review the entire unit through three sections.
• Vocabulary Practice: Learners can review the key words, phonics words, and sight words in the unit.
• Sentence Practice: Learners can practice reading and writing sentences from the passage.
• Reading Practice: Learners can check how well they understand the passage.

Scope and Sequence

My Family and I

Unit	Title	Subject	Genre
1	I Can	Social Studies	Nonfiction
2	I Am a Student	Social Studies	Nonfiction
3	I Love My Family	Social Studies	Fiction

Colors and Shapes

Unit	Title	Subject	Genre
4	I Need Red	Art	Fiction
5	Toys	Math	Fiction
6	Circles and Squares	Math	Nonfiction

Weather

Unit	Title	Subject	Genre
7	It Is Sunny	Science	Nonfiction
8	The Storm	Science	Fiction
9	My Skis	Literature	Fiction

Safety and Health

Unit	Title	Subject	Genre
10	Making Fruit Salad	Literature	Fiction
11	I Walk to School	Social Studies	Fiction
12	Riding a Bike	Physical Education	Fiction

 **LEXILE® BR90L–30L**

Key Words	Phonics	Build Language	Page
ride, swim, dance, wash, brush	c**a**n, d**a**nce	**I can** jump.	6
chef, nurse, farmer, soccer player, scientist	farm**er**, play**er**	**I am** a student.	14
mom, dad, sister, brother, family	**d**ad, **d**og	**I love** my dad.	22

Key Words	Phonics	Build Language	Page
red, orange, yellow, green, blue	n**ee**d, gr**ee**n	**I need** yellow.	30
ball, box, kite, puzzle, boat	tr**u**ck, p**u**zzle	**This is** a kite.	38
circle, square, rectangle, star, triangle	rectan**gle**, trian**gle**	**I have** one star.	46

Key Words	Phonics	Build Language	Page
sunny, hot, rainy, cold, snowy	sunn**y**, rain**y**	**It is** sunny.	54
sky, cloud, wind, lightning, sun	**s**ky, **s**un	**Look at** the sky.	62
pants, coat, boot, mitten, medal	**m**itten, **m**edal	**I put on** my coat.	70

Key Words	Phonics	Build Language	Page
pear, banana, blueberry, strawberry, melon	**p**ear, **p**ineapple	**We like** pears.	78
see, sign, car, light, safe	s**i**gn, b**i**ke	**I see** the school.	86
bike, helmet, fall, cut, bandage	**h**elmet, **h**orn	**She has** a bike.	94

I Can

Get Ready   What can he do?

My Family and I

Key Words

A Listen and repeat the words.

ride

swim

dance

wash

brush

Sight Words

I, can

B Check the correct words.

1.
☐ ride
☐ dance

2.
☐ swim
☐ brush

I Can

21 words

I can jump.

I can ride.

8

I can swim.

I can dance.

Check
Can the girl dance? [Yes] [No]

I can wash.

I can brush.

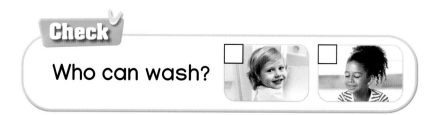

Check

Who can wash?

Find & Draw

I = ◯
can = △

I can read.

Aa Phonics Chant

a a a can
a a a dance
can can can
dance dance dance

Write & Read

 d__nce

 c__n

A **Choose the correct answers.**

1. I can ride. **a**  **b**

2.

I can **a** read .

b brush .

B **Choose and write the correct words.**

dance   wash   swim

1.

2.

3.

_____

_____

_____

C **Trace, find, and color.** = I = can

1. I

2. can

Read and chant. Then, trace.

♪ Chant

| I |
| I | can |
| I | can | jump | . |

| I | can | dance | . |

Retell Point, read, and say.

ride

jump

dance

swim

I can _____.

On Your Own What can you do?

Social Studies

2

Phonics: er
farmer, player

I Am a Student

Get Ready Who is she?

My Family and I

Key Words

A Listen and repeat the words.

Word Chant

chef

nurse

farmer

soccer player

Sight Words

am, a

scientist

B Circle the correct words.

1.

chef | farmer

2.

nurse | scientist

I Am a Student

25 words

I am a **chef**.

I am a **nurse**.

Check
Who is a chef? Circle him or her.

I am a **farmer**.

I am a **soccer player**.

Check

She 🧑 is a farmer. [Yes] [No]

Find & Draw

am = ☆
a = ▭

I am a **scientist**.

I am a student.

er **Phonics Chant**

er er er farmer
er er er player
farmer farmer farmer
player player player

Read & Circle

er

farmer

scientist

player

Reading Comprehension

A Choose the correct answers.

1.

I am a _____.

ⓐ scientist   ⓑ student

2.

I am a nurse. [Yes] [No]

B Choose and write the correct words.

1.

nurse

soccer player

2.

chef

scientist

3.

farmer

student

Sight Words

C Trace, find, and count.

1. am  am ☐

2. a a ☐

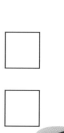

20

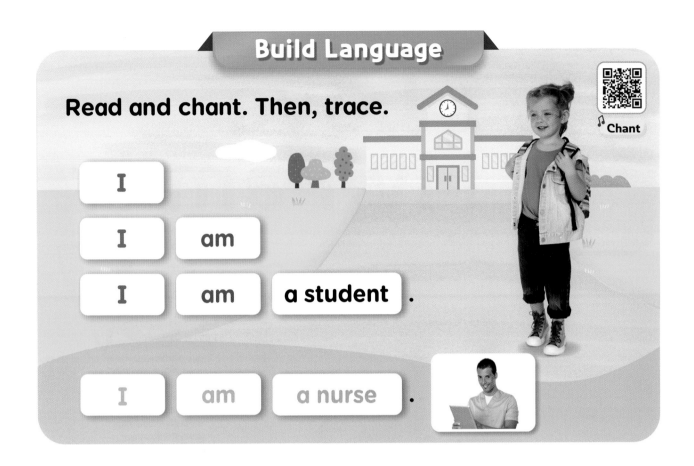

Build Language

Read and chant. Then, trace.

♪ Chant

I

I am

I am a student .

I am a nurse .

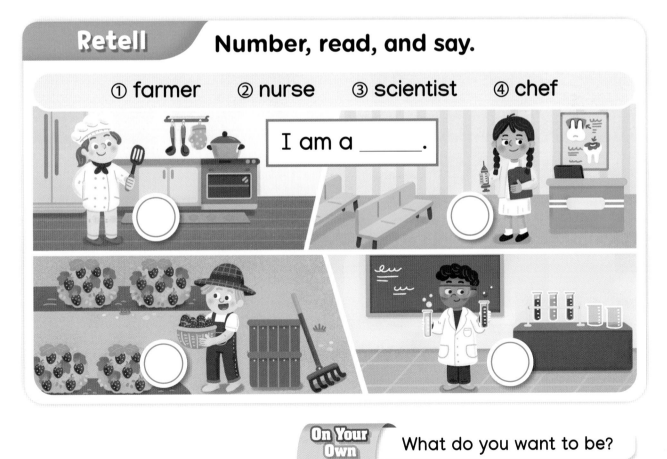

Retell   Number, read, and say.

① farmer   ② nurse   ③ scientist   ④ chef

I am a _____.

On Your Own   What do you want to be?

Social Studies

3

Phonics: d
dad, dog

I Love My Family

My Family and I

Get Ready Who are they?

A Listen and repeat the words.

🎵 **Word Chant**

mom

dad

sister

brother

family

Sight Words

love, my

B Check the correct words.

1.
☐ sister
☐ brother

2.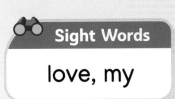
☐ mom
☐ dad

I Love My Family

24 words

Who does the boy love?

I love my mom.

I love my dad.

Check

What does his dad have?

I love my sister.

I love my brother.

Check

I  have 3 family members. [Yes] [No]

Find & Draw

love = ♡

my = ◎

I love my dog.
I love my family.

Dd

Phonics Chant

d d d dad
d d d dog
dad dad dad
dog dog dog

Write & Read

 __ad

 __og

A **Choose the correct answers.**

1. I  love my **ⓐ**

cat

ⓑ

dog .

2.

    ⓐ I love my dad.

    ⓑ I love my sister.

B **Write the correct words.**

1.

omm

2.

therbro

3.

ilyfam

Sight Words

C **Trace, find, and circle.**

1. love ----- love -----

2. my ----- my -----

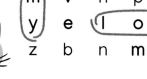

```
z  l  g  m  y  e  r
s  o  g  e  r  a  m
m  v  h  p  x  d  y
y  e  l  o  v  e  d
z  b  n  m  y  x  a
```

Read and chant. Then, trace.

I

I love

I love my dad .

I love my sister .

Retell Point, read, and say.

I love my _____.

mom

I

sister

brother

dad

On Your Own Who do you love in your family?

Art

4

Phonics: ee
need, green

I Need Red

Get Ready What colors do you see?

Colors and Shapes

30

A Listen and repeat the words.

 ♪ Word **Chant**

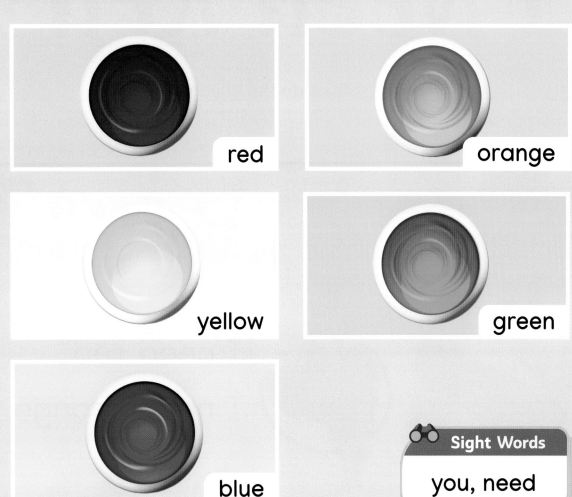

red

orange

yellow

green

blue

Sight Words

you, need

B Circle the correct words.

1.

| red | orange |

2.

| blue | green |

I Need Red

21 words

What colors do the children need?

I need red.

I need orange.

♪ Story Song

I need yellow.
You need green.

Check
The boy needs green. Yes No

I need white.

I need blue.

Check

What color does the girl  need?

34

Find & Draw

you = ◯
need = △

You need pink.

ee **Phonics Chant**

ee ee ee need
ee ee ee green
need need need
green green green

Read & Circle

ee

need

red

green

Reading Comprehension

A **Choose the correct answers.**

1. I need orange.

2.

You need
ⓐ pink .
ⓑ white .

B **Choose and write the correct words.**

green   yellow   red

1.

_____

2.

_____

3.

_____

Sight Words

C **Trace, find, and color.** = you   = need

1. you   you

2. need   need

Read and chant. Then, trace.

I

I need

I need **yellow** .

I need green .

Retell   **Number, read, and say.**

① orange   ② green   ③ blue   ④ red

I need _____.

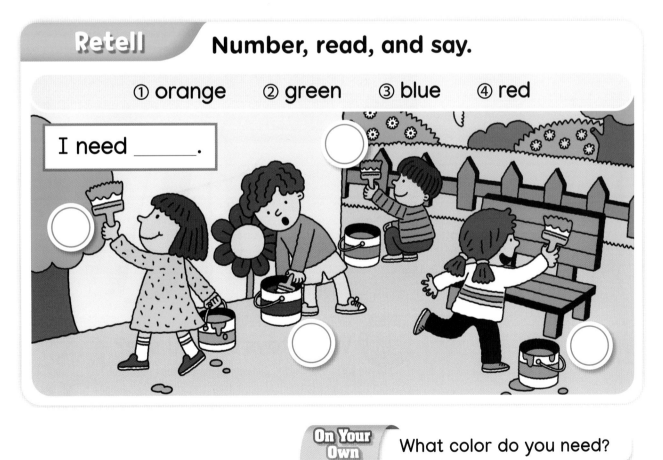

On Your Own   What color do you need?

Get Ready What toys do you see?

Colors and Shapes

A **Listen and repeat the words.**

♫ **Word Chant**

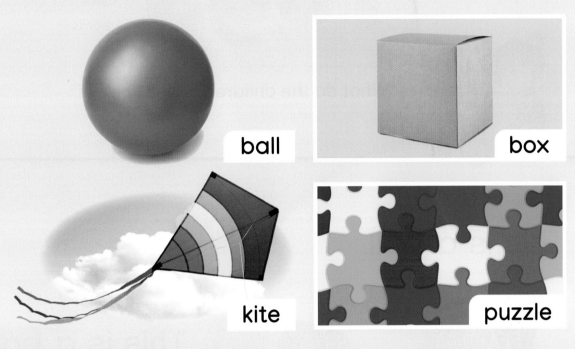

ball

box

kite

puzzle

boat

Sight Words

this, is

B **Check the correct words.**

1.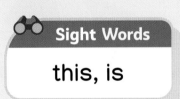
☐ kite
☐ puzzle

2.
☐ ball
☐ boat

Toys

24 words

Focus

What do the children have?

This is a **ball**.

This is a **box**.

This is a truck.

Check
Who has a ball? Circle him or her.

This is a kite.

This is a puzzle.

Check

What does he have?

42

Read and color!
① ② ③

Find & Draw
this = ☆
is = ▢

This is a boat.

Uu | **Phonics Chant** | **Write & Read**

u u u truck
u u u puzzle
truck truck truck
puzzle puzzle puzzle

 tr__ck

 p__zzle

A Choose the correct answers.

1.

This is a _____.
  ⓐ box   ⓑ puzzle

2.

This is a kite. (Yes) (No)

B Choose and write the correct words.

1.

box
boat
_____

2.

kite
ball
_____

3.

truck
puzzle
_____

Sight Words

C Trace, find, and count.

1. this   this   ☐

2. is   is   ☐

this
is   I   my   is   this
is   is   you
I
you   my
this   I

Read and chant. Then, trace.

This

This is

This is a kite .

This is a boat .

Retell Point, read, and say.

kite

puzzle

box

ball

This is a _____.

On Your Own What toys do you have?

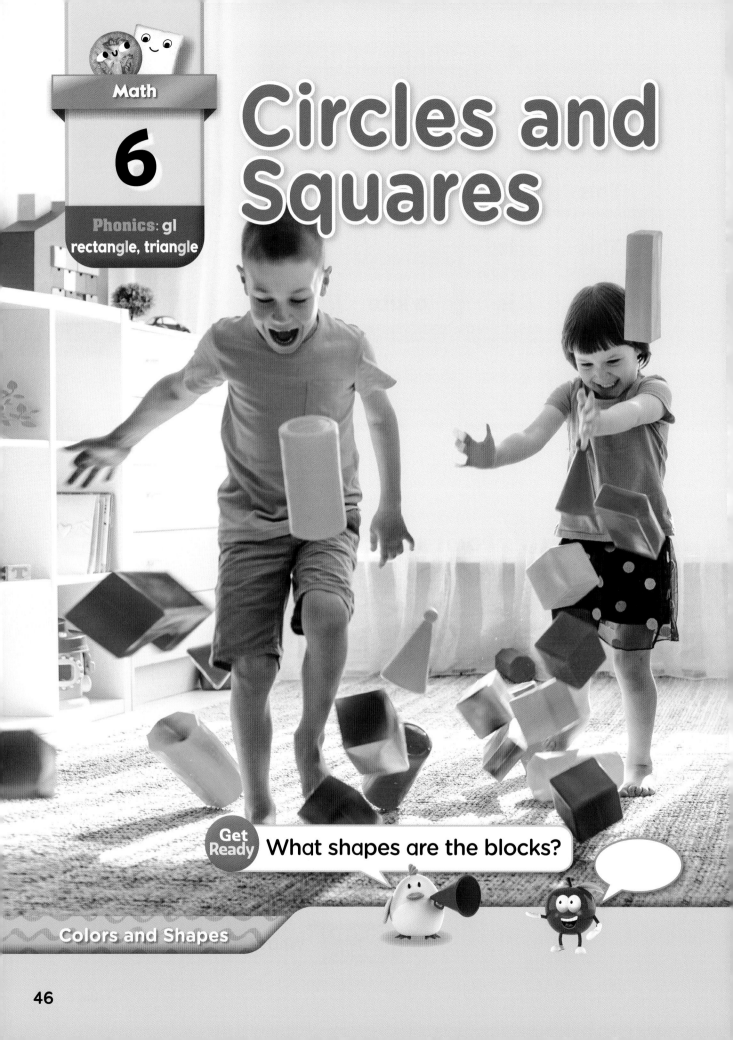

6

Circles and Squares

Get Ready What shapes are the blocks?

Colors and Shapes

♫ Word **Chant**

A **Listen and repeat the words.**

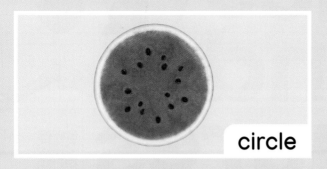
circle

square

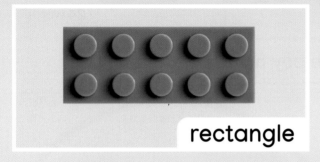
rectangle

star

triangle

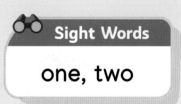
Sight Words
one, two

B **Circle the correct words.**

1.

star | circle

2.

square | rectangle

Circles and Squares

24 words

• Focus •
What shapes does the boy have?

I have one circle.

♫ Story Song

I have two squares.

I have two rectangles.

Check

The boy 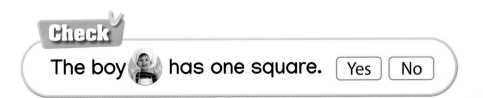 has one square. [Yes] [No]

I have two circles.

I have one star.

Check

What has a star shape? Circle it.

50

I have two **triangles**.

 gl | **Phonics Chant**

gl gl gl   rectangle
gl gl gl   triangle
rectangle   rectangle   rectangle
triangle   triangle   triangle

Read & Circle

gl

 circle

triangle

 rectangle

Reading Comprehension

A **Choose the correct answers.**

1. I  have two ⓐ  stars ⓑ  rectangles .

2.

ⓐ I have two squares.

ⓑ I have two triangles.

B **Write the correct words.**

1.

clecir

_____

_____

2.

tanglerec

_____

_____

3.

angletri

_____

_____

C **Trace, find, and circle.**

1. one ---- one ----

2. two ---- two ----

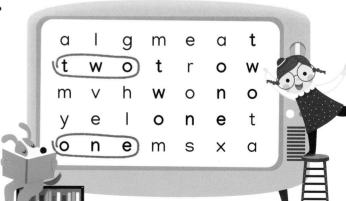

```
a  l  g  m  e  a  t
t  w  o  t  r  o  w
m  v  h  w  o  n  o
y  e  l  o  n  e  t
o  n  e  m  s  x  a
```

Read and chant. Then, trace.

I

I have

I have one star.

I have one circle.

Retell **Number, read, and say.**

① one circle ② two triangles ③ one rectangle ④ two stars

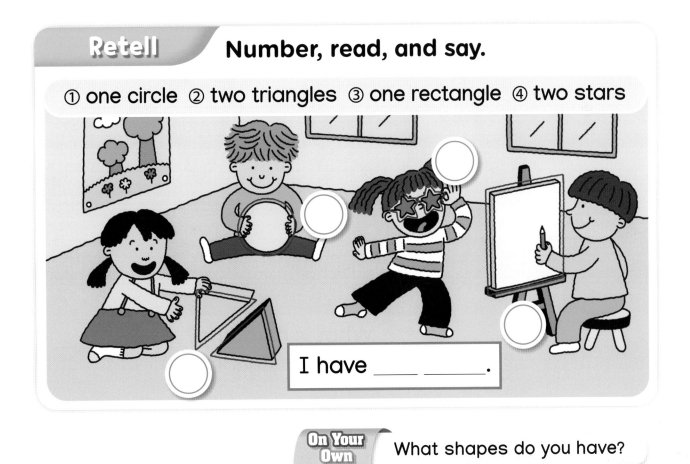

I have ____ ____.

On Your Own What shapes do you have?

7 It Is Sunny

Phonics: y
sunny, rainy

Weather

Get Ready What is he doing?

Key Words

A Listen and repeat the words.

♫ Word Chant

sunny

hot

rainy

cold

snowy

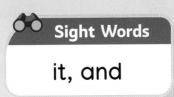
Sight Words

it, and

B Check the correct words.

1.
☐ rainy
☐ sunny

2.
☐ hot
☐ cold

It Is Sunny

25 words

Focus

What is the weather like?

It is sunny.
It is hot.

It is cloudy and windy.
It is cool.

Check

It is hot on sunny days. Yes No

It is rainy.

It is stormy.

Check

How is it on snowy days? [Hot] [Cold]

Find & Draw

it = ○
and = △

It is cold and snowy.

Yy Phonics Chant

y y y sunny
y y y rainy
sunny sunny sunny
rainy rainy rainy

Write & Read

 rain__

 sunn__

A **Choose the correct answers.**

1. It is stormy. ⓐ  ⓑ

2.  It is ⓐ cool .
ⓑ hot .

B **Choose and write the correct words.**

snowy   rainy   hot

1.
_____

2.
_____

3.
_____

Sight Words

C **Trace, find, and color.** = it   = and

1. it   _____it_____

2. and   _____and_____

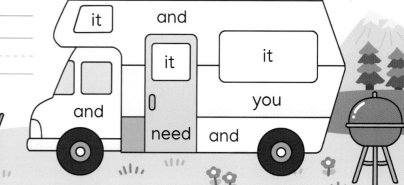

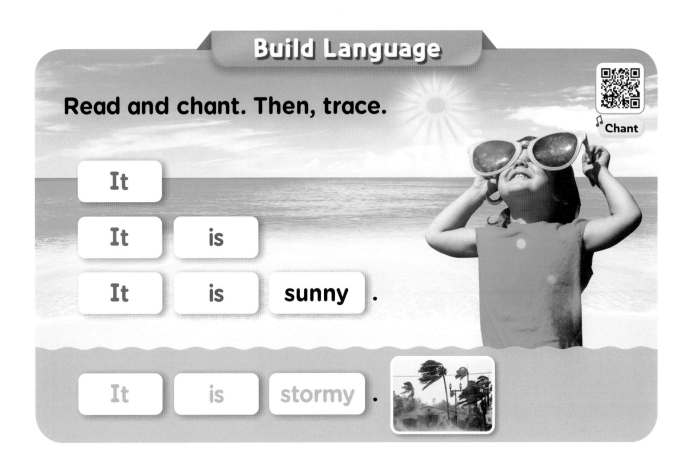

Build Language

Read and chant. Then, trace.

♪ Chant

It

It is

It is **sunny** .

It is stormy .

Retell Point, read, and say.

sunny

rainy

snowy

cold

It is _____ .

On Your Own How is the weather?

8

The Storm

Get Ready What's happening in the sea?

Weather

♪ **Word Chant**

A **Listen and repeat the words.**

sky

cloud

wind

lightning

sun

Sight Words

look, at

B **Circle the correct words.**

1.

cloud   sun

2.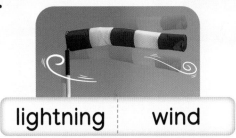

lightning   wind

The Storm

26 words

What is the boy looking at?

Look at the sky.

Story Song

Look at the clouds.

Look at the wind.

Check

The boy looks at the sky. Yes No

Look at the lightning.

Look at the rain.

Check

How does the boy feel at the end?

Find & Draw

look = ☆
at = ▢

Look at the sun.

I'm happy.

Ss **Phonics Chant**

s   s   s   sky
s   s   s   sun
sky   sky   sky
sun   sun   sun

Read & Circle

s

 sun

 rain

 sky

A Choose the correct answers.

1.

Look at the _____.

ⓐ lightning   ⓑ clouds

2.

Look at the rain. Yes   No

B Choose and write the correct words.

1.

sun
cloud
_____
_ _ _ _ _ _ _ _ _ _ _
_____

2.

wind
lightning
_____
_ _ _ _ _ _ _ _ _ _ _
_____

3.

sky
rain
_____
_ _ _ _ _ _ _ _ _ _ _
_____

Sight Words

C Trace, find, and count.

1. look   look   ☐

2. at   at   ☐

it
look   at
look   look   can
look   at   a
my   at   look   at
at   a

Read and chant. Then, trace.

Chant

Look

Look | at

Look | at | **the sky** .

Look | at | the sun .

Retell | Number, read, and say.

① lightning ② sky ③ sun ④ cloud

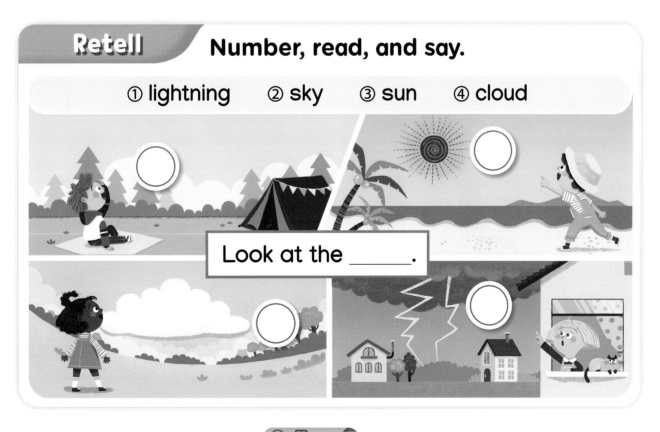

Look at the _____.

On Your Own What do you want to look at?

9

Phonics: m
mitten, medal

My Skis

Get Ready What are they wearing?

Weather

♪ Word Chant

A Listen and repeat the words.

pants

coat

boot

mitten

medal

Sight Words

put, on

B Check the correct words.

1.
☐ mitten
☐ medal

2.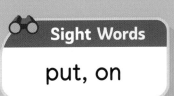
☐ coat
☐ pants

My Skis

25 words

What does Andy put on?

I put on my pants.

I put on my coat.

I put on my boots.

Check

He  puts on his pants. Yes No

I put on my mittens.

What sport does he do? ☐ ☐

74

Find & Draw

put = ♡
on = ◎

I put on my medal!

Mm **Phonics Chant**

m m m mitten
m m m medal
mitten mitten mitten
medal medal medal

Write & Read

 __itten

 __edal

Reading Comprehension

A **Choose the correct answers.**

1. I  put on my
   ⓐ  scarf
   ⓑ  boots .

2.
   ⓐ I put on my coat.
   ⓑ I put on my medal.

B **Write the correct words.**

1.

   ttensmi

   _____

2.

   tsboo

   _____

3.

   tspan

   _____

C **Trace, find, and circle.**

1. put   put

2. on   on

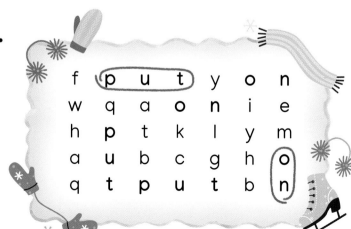

f (p u t) y o n
w q a o n i e
h p t k l y m
a u b c g h (o)
q t p u t b (n)

Read and chant. Then, trace.

♪ Chant

I

I put on

I put on my coat .

I put on my mittens .

Retell Point, read, and say.

I put on my _____ .

coat

boots

pants

mittens

On Your Own What do you put on?

10

Phonics: p
pear, pineapple

Making Fruit Salad

Safety and Health

Get Ready What fruit can you see?

♪ **Word Chant**

Ⓐ Listen and repeat the words.

pear

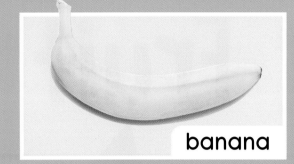
banana

blueberry

strawberry

melon

Sight Words

we, like

Ⓑ Circle the correct words.

1.

| banana | strawberry |

2.

| pear | melon |

Making Fruit Salad

26 words

We like oranges.

We like pears.

80

Story Song

We like bananas.

We like blueberries.

Check

They like pears. [Yes] [No]

We like strawberries.

We like melons.

We like pineapples.

Check

What fruit do they like?

This is our fruit salad.

Pp | **Phonics Chant**

p p p pear
p p p pineapple
pear pear pear
pineapple pineapple pineapple

Read & Circle

p

pear

pineapple

banana

Reading Comprehension

A **Choose the correct answers.**

1. We like oranges. **a**  **b**

2.  We like **a** pineapples .
   b strawberries .

B **Choose and write the correct words.**

banana   blueberry   melon

1.

_____

_____

2.

_____

_____

3.

_____

_____

Sight Words

C **Trace, find, and color.** = we   = like

1. we   we

2. like   like

Read and chant. Then, trace.

♪ Chant

We

We like

We like pears .

We like strawberries .

Retell Number, read, and say.

① pears ② bananas ③ blueberries ④ strawberries

We like _____ .

On Your Own   What fruit do you like?

I Walk to School

Get Ready How is she going to school?

Safety and Health

A Listen and repeat the words.

♫ Word Chant

see

sign

car

light

safe

Sight Words

see, the

B Check the correct words.

1.
☐ sign
☐ light

2.
☐ see
☐ safe

I walk to School

26 words

Focus

What does the boy see?

I see the sign.

I see the car.

I see the light.

I see the bike.

Check

I 🙂 see the light. ☐ 🚦 ☐ 🛑

I see the children.

Ii

Phonics Chant

i i i   sign
i i i   bike
sign sign sign
bike bike bike

Write & Read

 b__ke

 s__gn

90

Find & Draw
see = ☆
the = ▭

I see the school.

I'm safe.

Check

Where is the boy  going?

☐ ☐

A **Choose the correct answers.**

1.

I see the _____.

ⓐ school   ⓑ children

2.

I see the bike. [Yes] [No]

B **Choose and write the correct words.**

1.

car

bike

_____

_____

2.

sign

safe

_____

_____

3.

see

light

_____

_____

Sight Words

C **Trace, find, and count.**

1. see   see   [ ]

2. the   the   [ ]

can
the   the
    see
see   the   a   like
do   see
    see

Read and chant. Then, trace.

🎵 Chant

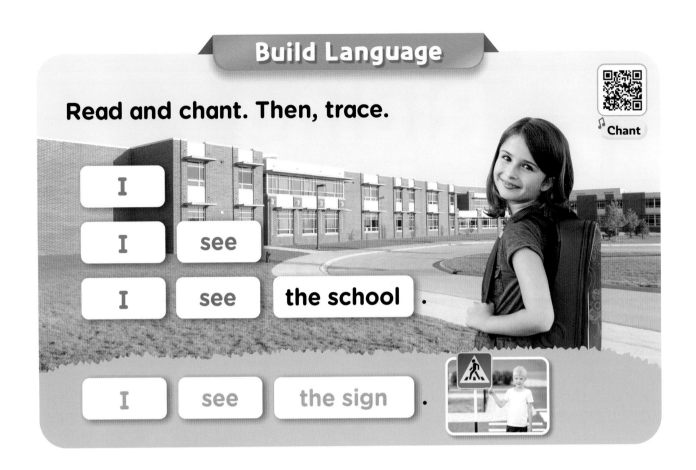

I

I | see

I | see | **the school** .

I | see | the sign .

Retell **Point, read, and say.**

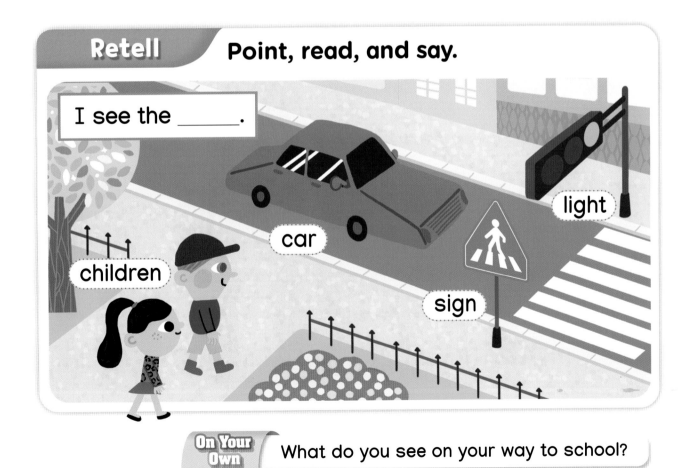

I see the _____.

light

car

children

sign

On Your Own What do you see on your way to school?

12

Phonics: h
helmet, horn

Riding a Bike

Get Ready What is he riding?

Safety and Health

94

🎵 Word Chant

A Listen and repeat the words.

bike

helmet

fall

cut

bandage

Sight Words

she, has

B Circle the correct words.

1.

bike | helmet

2.

cut | bandage

Riding a Bike

26 words

● Focus ●

What does the girl have?

She has a bike.

♪ Story Song

She has a helmet.

She has a horn.

Check

She has a bike. [Yes] [No]

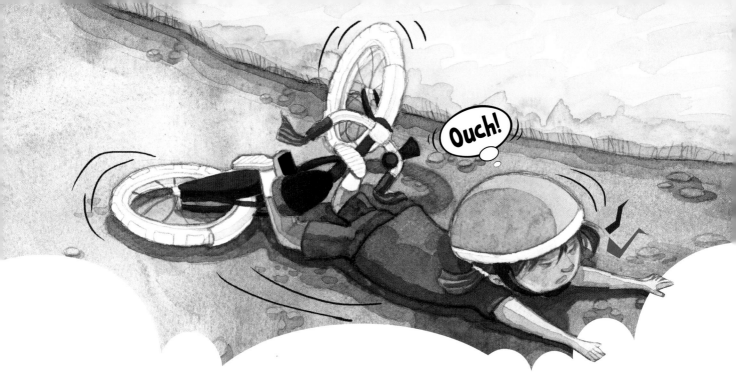

She falls.

She has a cut.

Phonics Chant

h h h helmet
h h h horn
helmet helmet helmet
horn horn horn

Read & Circle

h

 helmet

 bike

 horn

98

She has a **bandage**.

She is okay now.

Check

Who has a cut?

Reading Comprehension

A Choose the correct answers.

1. She  has a ⓐ  car ⓑ  horn .

2.

ⓐ She falls.

ⓑ She is okay now.

B Write the correct words.

1.  llfa

_____

_____

2.  tcu

_____

_____

3.  methel

_____

_____

Sight Words

C Trace, find, and circle.

1. she ----- she

2. has ----- has

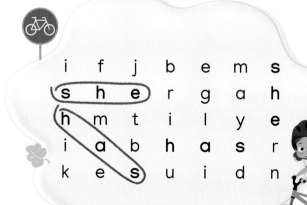

```
i  f  j  b  e  m  s
s  h  e  r  g  a  h
h  m  t  i  l  y  e
i  a  b  h  a  s  r
k  e  s  u  i  d  n
```

Build Language

Read and chant. Then, trace.

♪ Chant

She

She | has

She | has | a bike .

She | has | a cut .

Retell   **Number, read, and say.**

① cut ② helmet ③ bike ④ bandage

She has a _____ .

On Your Own   What do you have?

Word List

Unit 1

 brush

 dance

 ride

 swim

 wash

Unit 2

 chef

 farmer

 nurse

 scientist

 soccer player

Unit 3

 brother

 dad

 family

 mom

 sister

Unit 4

 blue

 green

 orange

 red

 yellow

Unit 5

 ball

 boat

 box

 kite

 puzzle

Unit 6

 circle

 rectangle

 square

 star

 triangle

Unit 7

 cold

 hot

 rainy

 snowy

 sunny

Unit 8

 cloud

 lightning

 sky

 sun

 wind

Unit 9

 boot

 coat

 medal

 mitten

 pants

Unit 10

 banana

 blueberry

 melon

 pear

 strawberry

Unit 11

 car

 light

 safe

 see

 sign

Unit 12

 bandage

 bike

 cut

 fall

 helmet

Photo Credits

20 words

Benchmark Reading

WORKBOOK

Starter 1

BR90L-30L

20 words

Benchmark Reading

Starter 1

WORKBOOK

Benchmark EDUCATION

Building Literacy and Language for Life ™

Vocabulary Practice

A Read and write the words twice.

1. ride
2. swim
3. dance
4. wash
5. brush

B Circle the word that doesn't have a short "a" sound.

dance   brush   can

C Read, trace, and write the sight words.

1. I   I

2. can   can

Sentence Practice

D Unscramble the words to complete the sentences.

1. I can

jump.

2. I

can   dance.

3. I

brush.   can

Reading Practice

E Read the sentences and match the correct pictures.

1. I can read. •

• ⓐ

2. I can swim. •

• ⓑ

3. I can wash. •

• ⓒ

2 I Am a Student

Vocabulary Practice

A **Read and write the words twice.**

1. chef

2. nurse

3. farmer

4. soccer player

5. scientist

B **Circle the word that doesn't have an "er" sound.**

read   farmer   player

C **Read, trace, and write the sight words.**

1. am   am

2. a   a

Sentence Practice

D **Unscramble the words to complete the sentences.**

1.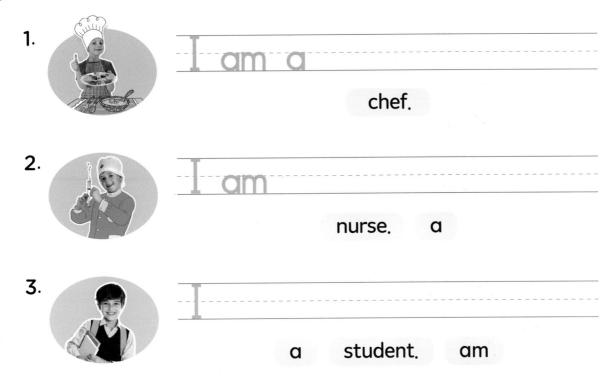

I am a

chef.

2.

I am

nurse.   a

3.

I

a   student.   am

Reading Practice

E **Read the sentences and match the correct pictures.**

1. I am a farmer.   •

•ⓐ

2. I am a scientist.   •

•ⓑ

3. I am a soccer player. •

•ⓒ

I Love My Family

A Read and write the words twice.

1. mom

2. dad

3. sister

4. brother

5. family

B Circle the word that doesn't have a "d" sound.

dog   dad   brother

C Read, trace, and write the sight words.

1. love   love

2. my   my

Sentence Practice

D Unscramble the words to complete the sentences.

1. I love my

    mom.

2. I love

    my   brother.

3. I

    love   dog.   my

Reading Practice

E Read the sentences and match the correct pictures.

1. I love my dad. •

    • ⓐ

2. I love my sister. •

    • ⓑ

3. I love my family. •

    • ⓒ

4 I Need Red

Vocabulary Practice

A Read and write the words twice.

1. red

2. orange

3. yellow

4. green

5. blue

B Circle the word that doesn't have an "ee" sound.

 need   green   blue

C Read, trace, and write the sight words.

1. you   you

2. need   need

8

D **Unscramble the words to complete the sentences.**

1.

I need _____

red.

2.

I _____

orange.   need

3.

You _____

need   pink.

E **Read the sentences and match the correct pictures.**

1. I need blue.   •

• ⓐ

2. I need yellow.   •

• ⓑ

3. You need green.   •

• ⓒ

5 Toys

A Read and write the words twice.

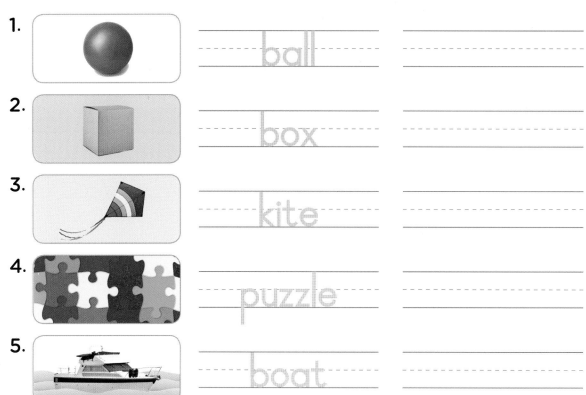

1. ball

2. box

3. kite

4. puzzle

5. boat

B Circle the word that doesn't have a short "u" sound.

truck   kite   puzzle

C Read, trace, and write the sight words.

1. this   this

2. is   is

D **Unscramble the words to complete the sentences.**

1. This is a
ball.

2. This is
box.   a

3. This
a   puzzle.   is

E **Read the sentences and match the correct pictures.**

1. This is a kite. •

• ⓐ

2. This is a boat. •

• ⓑ

3. This is a truck. •

• ⓒ

6 Circles and Squares

A Read and write the words twice.

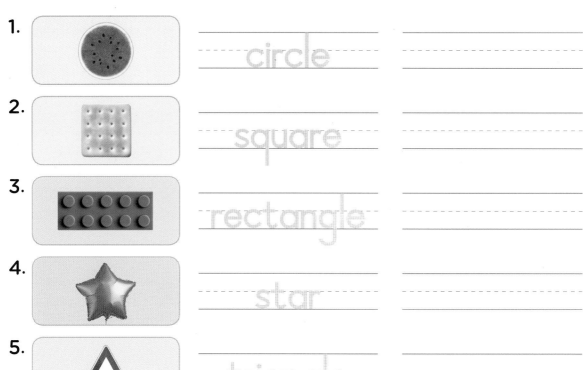

1. circle

2. square

3. rectangle

4. star

5. triangle

B Circle the word that doesn't have a "gl" sound.

blue   rectangle   triangle

C Read, trace, and write the sight words.

1. one   one

2. two   two

D **Unscramble the words to complete the sentences.**

1. I have two

rectangles.

2. I have

two   circles.

3. I

have   star.   one

E **Read the sentences and match the correct pictures.**

1. I have one circle.   •

•ⓐ

2. I have two squares.   •

•ⓑ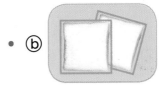

3. I have two triangles.   •

•ⓒ

7 It Is Sunny

Vocabulary Practice

A Read and write the words twice.

1. sunny _____

2. hot _____

3. rainy _____

4. cold _____

5. snowy _____

B Circle the word that doesn't have a "y" sound.

ride   rainy   sunny

C Read, trace, and write the sight words.

1. it   it _____ _____

2. and   and _____ _____

Sentence Practice

D **Unscramble the words to complete the sentences.**

1. It is

    sunny.

2. It

    stormy.   is

3. It

    cloudy   is   windy.   and

Reading Practice

E **Read the sentences and match the correct pictures.**

1. It is hot.   •

    • ⓐ

2. It is rainy.   •

    • ⓑ

3. It is cold and snowy. •

    • ⓒ

8 The Storm

A Read and write the words twice.

1. sky
2. cloud
3. wind
4. lightning
5. sun

B Circle the word that doesn't have an "s" sound.

sky   sun   red

C Read, trace, and write the sight words.

1. look   look

2. at   at

16

Sentence Practice

D **Unscramble the words to complete the sentences.**

1.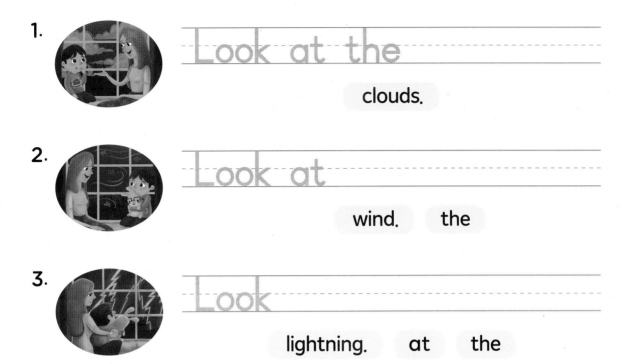

Look at the

clouds.

2. Look at

wind.   the

3. Look

lightning.   at   the

Reading Practice

E **Read the sentences and match the correct pictures.**

1. Look at the sky. •

• ⓐ

2. Look at the rain. •

• ⓑ

3. Look at the sun. •

• ⓒ

9 My Skis

Vocabulary Practice

A Read and write the words twice.

1. pants
2. coat
3. boot
4. mitten
5. medal

B Circle the word that doesn't have an "m" sound.

mitten   coat   medal

C Read, trace, and write the sight words.

1. put   put

2. on   on

18

Sentence Practice

D Unscramble the words to complete the sentences.

1.
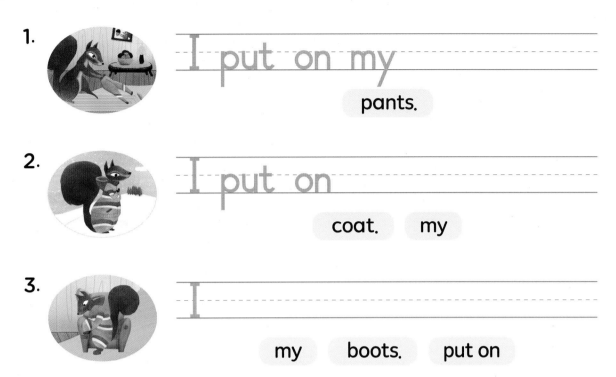

I put on my

pants.

2.

I put on

coat.   my

3.

I

my   boots.   put on

Reading Practice

E Read the sentences and match the correct pictures.

1. I put on my medal! •

•ⓐ

2. I put on my pants. •

•ⓑ

3. I put on my mittens. •

•ⓒ

10 Making Fruit Salad

Vocabulary Practice

A Read and write the words twice.

1. pear
2. banana
3. blueberry
4. strawberry
5. melon

B Circle the word that doesn't have a "p" sound.

<u>p</u>ineapple   <u>m</u>elon   <u>p</u>ear

C Read, trace, and write the sight words.

1. we   we

2. like   like

D **Unscramble the words to complete the sentences.**

1.  We like

   pears.

2. We

   like   bananas.

3. We

   strawberries.   like

Reading Practice

E **Read the sentences and match the correct pictures.**

1. We like melons.   •

   • ⓐ

2. We like oranges.   •

   • ⓑ

3. This is our fruit salad. •

   • ⓒ

I Walk to School

A **Read and write the words twice.**

1. see _____ _____

2. sign _____ _____

3. car _____ _____

4. light _____ _____

5. safe _____ _____

B **Circle the word that doesn't have a long "i" sound.**

sign   car   bike

C **Read, trace, and write the sight words.**

1. see   see _____ _____

2. the   the _____ _____

Sentence Practice

D **Unscramble the words to complete the sentences.**

1.

I see the

car.

2.

I see

light.   the

3.

I

the   school.   see

Reading Practice

E **Read the sentences and match the correct pictures.**

1. I'm safe.   •

• ⓐ

2. I see the bike.   •

• ⓑ

3. I see the children. •

• ⓒ

12 Riding a Bike

Vocabulary Practice

A Read and write the words twice.

1. bike

2. helmet

3. cut

4. fall

5. bandage

B Circle the word that doesn't have an "h" sound.

fall   horn   helmet

C Read, trace, and write the sight words.

1. she   she

2. has   has

D Unscramble the words to complete the sentences.

1. She has a

   bike.

2. She has

   helmet.   a

3. She

   a   horn.   has

E Read the sentences and match the correct pictures.

1. She has a cut.   •

   • ⓐ

2. She is okay now.   •

   • ⓑ

3. She has a bandage. •

   • ⓒ

· Make your own picture dictionary.

Unit 1

Unit 2

Unit 3

Unit 4

Unit 5

_____
- - - - - - - - - - - - -
_____

_____
- - - - - - - - - - - - -
_____

_____
- - - - - - - - - - - - -
_____

_____
- - - - - - - - - - - - -
_____

_____
- - - - - - - - - - - - -
_____

Unit 6

_____
- - - - - - - - - - - - -
_____

_____
- - - - - - - - - - - - -
_____

_____
- - - - - - - - - - - - -
_____

_____
- - - - - - - - - - - - -
_____

_____
- - - - - - - - - - - - -
_____

Unit 7

_____
- - - - - - - - - - - - -
_____

_____
- - - - - - - - - - - - -
_____

_____
- - - - - - - - - - - - -
_____

_____
- - - - - - - - - - - - -
_____

_____
- - - - - - - - - - - - -
_____

Unit 8

_____
- - - - - - - - - - - - -
_____

_____
- - - - - - - - - - - - -
_____

_____
- - - - - - - - - - - - -
_____

_____
- - - - - - - - - - - - -
_____

_____
- - - - - - - - - - - - -
_____

_____

_____

_____

_____

_____

_____

_____

_____

_____

_____

_____

_____

_____

_____

_____

_____

_____

_____

_____

_____